LIVING WITH
DEAFNESS

Emma Haughton

WAYLAND

Titles in the series

Living with Asthma

Living with Blindness

Living with Cerebral Palsy

Living with Deafness

Living with Diabetes

Living with Down's Syndrome

Living with Epilepsy

Living with Leukaemia

Editor: Carron Brown
Picture research: Gina Brown
Cover design: Steve Wheele Design
Book designer: Peter Laws
Consultant: Nick Tapp, Deputy Chief Executive, East Sussex Disability Association

First published in 1999 by Wayland Publishers Ltd, 61 Western Road, Hove,
East Sussex, BN3 1JD, England

Find Wayland on the Internet at http://www.wayland.co.uk

British Library in Publication Data
Haughton, Emma
   Living with Deafness
   1. Deafness – Juvenile literature
   2. Deaf – Juvenile literature
   I. Title
   362.1'978

ISBN 0 7502 2389 8

Printed and bound in Italy by G. Canale and C.S.p.A.

Picture acknowledgements
Wayland Publishers would like to thank: John Birdsall 11 (top), 17, 27; Eye
Ubiquitous/Paul Seheult 24; Sally and Richard Greenhill *cover* (bottom) 7, 25, 26;
Science Photo Library/ Bo Veisland, MI&I 6, /Simon Fraser (Brompton Day Hospital,
Cumbria) 7; Trip/S. Grant 19; Wayland Picture Library 16, /Angus Blackburn *cover*
(main), 28, /Martin F. Chillmaid title page, 4–5, 8, 9, 12–15, 18, 21–3, 29, 31, /Tim
Woodcock *cover* (top); Zefa 11 (bottom), /Ed Bock 10.

We would like to thank the following schools for their help with this project:
Braidwood (School for the Deaf), Perry Common Road, Birmingham B23 7AT; Howes
School, Palermo Avenue, Coventry; and St Thomas Moore R C First School, Studley
Road, Redditch B98 7YR.

The National Deaf Children's Society (NDCS) and the Royal National Institute for
Deaf People (RNID) were consulted throughout the preparation of this book.

Contents

Meet Tom, Gita, Alison and Alfred

Tom, Gita, Alison and Alfred look the same as everyone else, although they are all deaf. Unless someone wears a hearing aid or uses sign language, you can't easily tell that he or she is deaf.

Like many young children, Tom had 'glue ear', a kind of blockage in his ears caused by fluid. When he was little, Tom had trouble keeping up with lessons at school because it was difficult for him to hear his teachers.

▷ Gita is determined that her deafness will not stop her enjoying life.

Gita goes to the same school as her hearing brothers, even though she has been severely deaf since she had meningitis. By wearing a hearing aid and reading people's lips, Gita manages well at school. She has many hearing friends.

◁ Tom has a lot of friends, but sometimes he finds it difficult to hear what they are saying.

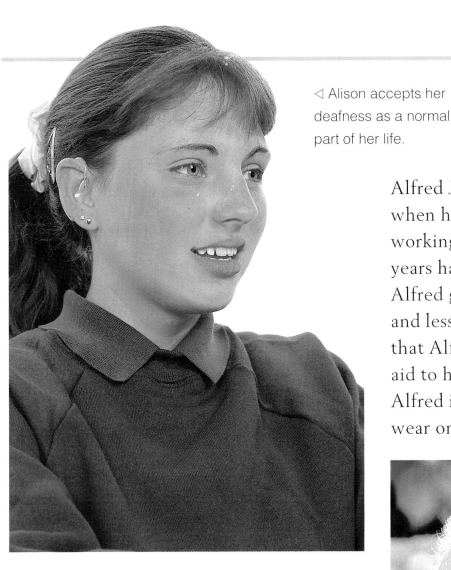

◁ Alison accepts her deafness as a normal part of her life.

Alfred Jones could hear very well when he was young. However, working in a noisy factory for many years has resulted in deafness. As Alfred grows older, he can hear less and less. His doctor has suggested that Alfred could wear a hearing aid to help him hear better, but Alfred is not sure if he wants to wear one.

Alison was born profoundly deaf and she hears very little, even when she wears a powerful hearing aid. She has never heard her own voice, and her speech is not as clear as that of her hearing friends. Although Alison can talk and lip-read, she prefers to communicate with her deaf friends at school using sign language.

▷ Alfred finds it difficult to accept his deafness.

What is deafness?

When someone has difficulty hearing, some people call it a hearing impairment, others prefer to use the word deaf.

Our ears enable us to detect a range of different sounds as well as speech, and our brain allows us to make sense of the sounds we hear. When sound waves enter the brain, they travel through the ear canal and cause the ear drum and the ting bones in the middle ear to vibrate. When these vibrations reach the inner ear, they stimulate the thousands of hair cells in the cochlea. The hair cells send an electrical message to the brain telling us what we hear.

▽ The ear is a complex and delicate part of the body.

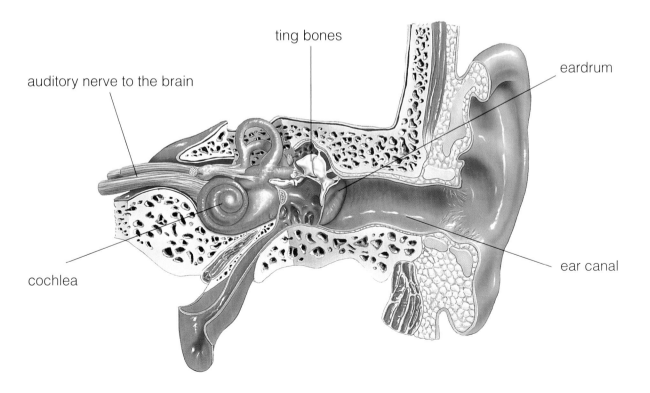

ting bones

auditory nerve to the brain

eardrum

ear canal

cochlea

▷ Many people need to use a hearing aid as they grow older.

There are different levels of hearing loss. Some people can hear loud sounds but not very quiet sounds. Some people can hear sounds that are low in pitch but not those that are high pitched. Very few people have no hearing.

There are many reasons why some people have difficulty hearing. Some people are born with a hearing problem. Sometimes it can be caused by illness. People often find it harder to hear as they grow older.

◁ In some cases, particularly when a child is born deaf, no one knows the reason why.

Managing deafness

Technology has helped many deaf children and adults. Many deaf people wear a hearing aid which helps them to hear more. Very few people are completely deaf and often a hearing aid can boost the amount of sound they can hear, though it can never restore hearing completely. The most common hearing aids are worn behind the ear, and are carefully chosen to match the amount and type of hearing loss of their user. Some hearing aids that fit right into the ear are very small and hard to see.

▽ Gita is so used to her hearing aid that she rarely notices she is wearing it.

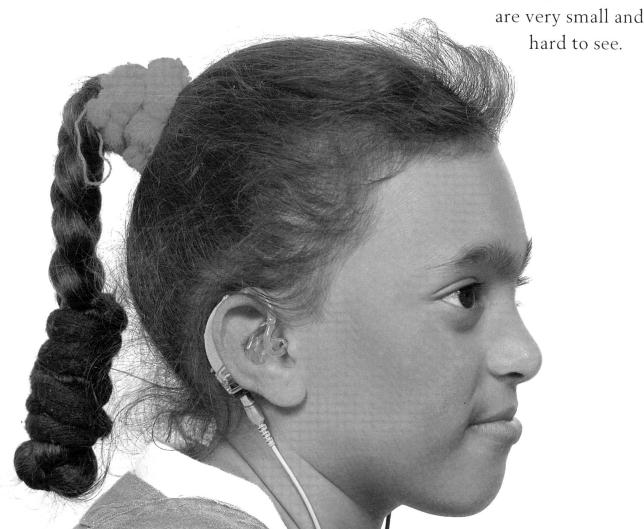

△ Like many deaf people, Tom often watches people's lips to understand what they are saying.

In recent years, doctors have been able to perform an operation to give very deaf people a cochlear implant, rather than a hearing aid. A cochlear implant is a device placed in the inner ear that sends signals to a tiny receiver placed under the skin behind the ear. Along with lip-reading, it can help deaf people understand what people are saying more easily.

Some types of deafness, may be temporary and disappear when a child grows. However, deafness has many different causes, and not all are easily managed. Many countries use vaccinations to help prevent diseases, such as mumps, measles and meningitis, that can sometimes cause deafness in children.

Aids to communication

Modern technology can be a big help for deaf people at home and at work. The Internet, for example, lets you talk to someone by typing into a computer rather than using a telephone. Subtitles allow deaf people to read what people are saying on television programmes.

Deaf people can now use the telephone more easily, with devices that make conversation louder or services that show what hearing people are saying as words on a screen. Deaf people can also talk to each other using a textphone, which is a special phone that allows you to type in messages rather than talk.

▽ Deaf people can use computers to communicate with someone instead of using a telephone.

△ Textphones help deaf people to communicate using the telephone.

◁ In the future, videophones may allow people to communicate by lip-reading and using sign language.

Noisy public places, such as banks and railway stations, can be difficult for people wearing hearing aids. There are devices that can help. Induction loops that cut out background noise and allow deaf people to tune into announcements and information through their aids. Other devices, such as vibrating or flashing alarms and bells, can warn of risks like fire, or let a deaf person know there is someone at the door.

Not all aids for deaf people rely on technology. Hearing dogs can help deaf people in much the same way as guide dogs aid blind people, by alerting their owners to possible dangers. For deaf people who use sign language, a sign language interpreter is often the most important aid to communication.

Growing up with deafness

When Tom was tested as a baby, he did not seem to be deaf, but Tom's parents noticed that as he grew older, Tom was slow to talk and often didn't seem to hear what people said. At school, Tom's teacher noticed he was having trouble with his work, and with speaking and listening in class.

Being careful

'I can hear clearly now, but I still have to be careful. When I go swimming, I have to keep my ears out of the water, which is quite difficult sometimes.'

▽ Tom's doctor detected his hearing problem by looking into his ears.

△ Tom finds it easier to talk to his friends in quiet places where he can hear them more clearly.

The family doctor examined Tom's ears and found that he had 'glue ear', a kind of thick fluid in his ears that stopped him hearing properly. The doctor explained it was like trying to hear through water. She said that the problem would go away, but Tom's hearing seemed to get worse. A hospital doctor decided that Tom needed an operation. Small plastic tubes called grommets were put into his ears to help drain away the fluid. Tom can now hear very well, but he has to be careful not to get water in his ears.

Some children who have a more serious hearing loss, or who are born deaf, find it difficult to learn to talk and manage in an ordinary school. Tom's hearing problems were mild and only lasted a few years. He did not find it too hard to catch up with his speech and school work.

Learning to communicate

When Alison was a baby, her parents noticed that she didn't seem to hear everyday sounds. After some tests, her doctor discovered that she was profoundly deaf. A teacher of deaf children came round to the family's house and showed Alison's parents how to help her learn to talk and communicate.

◁ Alison's communication skills developed well at her school.

Alison went to a school for deaf children when she was five years old. Although at home she had learned to understand a lot of what people were saying just by lip-reading, she found it very difficult to talk clearly herself. At school, Alison learnt to speak more clearly. Being in a school with a lot of other deaf children also helped her to develop sign language.

Using sign language

'My deaf friends and I prefer to use sign language to communicate with each other. It's easier to express your feelings and more relaxing than using speech.'

△ For Alison, gesture and sign language have always been the ways that she prefers to communicate.

Now Alison is a teenager, she can understand a lot of what people say to her, and her speech is quite clear. But Alison still finds lip-reading and talking very tiring, especially for long periods of time.

A deaf person in the family

◁ Sometimes deaf children feel they are not allowed to do things that their hearing brothers or sisters do, such as crossing a road, because their parents are worried about them.

Although some deaf children also have deaf parents, brothers or sisters, most deaf children are born into families where everyone else is hearing. This can be difficult for parents who may feel they have to give a lot of help and attention to their deaf child.

Being a deaf child in a hearing family can sometimes feel a bit lonely. You can feel left out of conversations that are going on around you. It is harder to join in games with your brothers and sisters if you find it difficult to understand what they are saying.

It can be hard for hearing children in the family, too. You may feel angry that your deaf brother or sister seems to get more attention from your parents, or you may get cross that your parents often expect you to help your deaf brother or sister. If the deaf child in your family doesn't use sign language, or if you find it difficult to learn how to sign, sometimes it can be frustrating trying to understand each other.

▽ Families often learn sign language to help communicate with a deaf family member.

Most families, however, learn ways to cope with these difficulties, and most deaf children can grow up feeling as much a part of the family as anyone else.

Going to school

Most deaf children go to ordinary schools with their hearing friends. Some can manage with just a hearing aid, but others like Gita use a radio aid to help them listen to what their teachers are saying.

Some deaf children also get special help in the classroom from an assistant or a teacher who is specially trained to help deaf pupils. Larger schools sometimes have a special unit for deaf children, where they can have some extra help from specially trained teachers. They may also have speech therapy there.

△ Gita's teacher wears a microphone that directs what he is saying straight to her hearing aid.

Children like Alison, who have very little hearing and need more support, can go to schools for deaf pupils. These schools have teachers who are specially trained to teach deaf children, and other people such as speech therapists who can help pupils with talking and understanding speech. Children who go to these schools are taught in small classes in classrooms that are less noisy than in ordinary schools. This makes it easier to use hearing aids well. As there are not very many of these schools, many deaf children have to live at their school during the week because it is too far to travel from home each day.

▽ With special help, deaf children can learn very quickly.

Attitudes to deaf people

Gita enjoys going to the same school as her hearing brothers and has plenty of hearing friends. When she first started school, she was the only deaf child there.

Although she loves making new friends, Gita doesn't always like the way people treat her. Sometimes they ignore her and talk to her parents and brothers instead. Sometimes they speak very slowly as if she were stupid, or they shout into her hearing aid, which hurts her ears. It can make Gita feel very angry and upset.

△ Gita's friends aren't bothered about her deafness.

Wearing a hearing aid

'At first, I found it hard when other children stared and asked me about my hearing aid, but now, no one seems to notice.'

Gita finds it easier to communicate well if people talk to her in a quiet place, and look straight at her so she can read their lips clearly. It also helps if they gesture and use facial expression. Gita understands most of what people say, but if she doesn't understand something, she needs to ask people to say it again. When she does get things wrong, it helps if people keep calm and say the same thing again in a slightly different way.

▽ Gita finds it easier to communicate with people if they look straight at her when they talk.

Missing sound

△ Alfred misses hearing the birds singing in his garden.

Alfred was not always deaf, but working for years in a noisy job and old age have gradually resulted in his hearing loss. Alfred finds his deafness very hard to accept. Unlike Alison, who has always been deaf, Alfred can remember quite clearly what it was like to hear well. It upsets him that he can no longer listen to his favourite music.

Alfred's doctor has suggested that he could wear a hearing aid, but Alfred has put it off for many years. Much of the time he prefers to think that his hearing is not really so bad. But Alfred is finding his deafness more and more difficult to manage. He finds it harder to understand what people are saying, and once was nearly hit by a speeding car that he couldn't hear approaching him. Unlike Alison, he has not developed other skills such as lip-reading to help him manage.

Those of us who hear well often take our ability for granted. It is easy to forget how much we rely on our hearing to help us in our daily lives.

◁ Alfred's hearing loss is now so bad that he often doesn't hear the phone ring.

Deaf people at work

Being deaf doesn't mean you can't work. Deaf people expect to have good job opportunities like everyone else. They have the ability to work in a wide range of jobs, particularly now that modern equipment and aids have removed many of the practical limitations that deaf people used to experience in the workplace. For example, textphones and computer technology make it possible for deaf people to work effectively in the business world.

▽ Companies often find it useful to have deaf staff who can communicate with deaf customers.

Deaf people now work in jobs ranging from carpentry to the computer industry, and you will meet them in offices, factories and television production units.

In many countries, such as the UK, the government encourages employers to employ and support deaf people. For example, some companies provide a textphone rather than an ordinary telephone, and may make lip-speakers and sign language interpreters available for meetings so that deaf people can follow what other people are saying. Some employers also provide training courses to help their hearing staff improve their communication skills with deaf people so that deaf and hearing people can work together more effectively.

△ Deaf people can do most jobs as well as their hearing colleagues.

Technology has helped many deaf people overcome practical difficulties in the workplace. Today, problems often result from the wrong attitudes and expectations of hearing people. Many people wrongly assume that deaf people cannot do a good job and do not give them a chance to try.

The deaf world

Hearing people often like to mix in noisy or dimly lit places such as pubs or clubs, but in these places it is very difficult for deaf people to lip-read or use hearing aids. Often deaf people feel more comfortable with each other, particularly if they use sign language. Around the world many local groups and clubs have sprung up to provide deaf people with more opportunities to meet.

▽ Clubs for deaf children can be a chance to improve sign language skills.

△ Deaf clubs offer a
chance to meet other
deaf people.

In many places, there is a deaf culture and community that
hearing people are often not even aware of. On the Internet,
for example, there are a lot of sites for deaf issues and
information.

You could almost say that deaf people are part of a huge
worldwide club. Sharing many problems and experiences in
life, deaf people of different nationalities often have much
more in common than hearing people. Although deafness
can be a barrier to communicate with hearing people, for
many deaf people in a hearing society, it is also a bond.

Getting help

Most countries have many people who can offer support to deaf people and their families. Regular hearing checks help doctors find deaf babies and children early, so that their parents can get the support they need to adapt to their child's deafness.

◁ Sometimes it is much easier to share your problems and worries with other people who have been through similar experiences.

There are also many organizations that can offer deaf people and parents plenty of advice, support and information about everything from treatment to special schools. They can bring deaf people and their families together so they can talk and support one another.

There are many deaf groups in the UK. Here are some you might like to contact:

- British Deaf Association (BDA), 1–3 Worship Street, London EC2A 2AB. Voice and text telephone: 0171 588 3520. Website: www.bda.org.uk
- Friends of Young Deaf People, East Court Mansion, Council Offices, College Lane, East Grinstead, RH19 3LT. Text: 01342 312639. Voice: 01342 323444.
- Hearing Concern, 11 Armstrong Road, London W3 7JL. Voice and text telephone: 0181 743 1110. Website: http://web.ukonline.co.uk/hearing-concern
- The National Deaf Children's Society (NDCS), 15 Dufferin Street, London EC1Y 8UR. Voice and text helpline: 0171 250 0123. Fax 0171 251 5020.

The NDCS is an organization of families, parents and carers which exists to enable deaf children and young people to make the most of their skills and abilities. Through their national and regional staff they provide a range of services throughout the UK. Local groups offer activities for families and a chance to meet other parents. NDCS provides information and advice on all aspects of childhood deafness – from books to benefits and education to equipment.

- The Royal National Institute for Deaf People (RNID), 19–23 Featherstone Street, London EC1Y 8SL or telephone 0171 296 8000 (voice) or 0171 296 8001 (text). Website: www.rnid.org.uk

The work of the RNID is described as follows: The Royal National Institute for Deaf People (RNID) is the largest charity representing the 8.7 million deaf and hard of hearing people in the UK. As a membership charity, we aim to achieve a radically better quality to life for deaf and hard of hearing people. We do this by campaigning and lobbying vigorously; by raising awareness of deafness and hearing loss; by providing services and through social, medical and technical research.

Glossary

Cochlea The hearing part of the inner ear.

Communication The ways with which people keep in touch, and pass on ideas and feelings to others.

Fluid Something that is not solid, such as water.

Gesture The movement of the body to express feeling
.
Glue ear Thick fluid in the ear.

Grommets Small plastic tubes that are placed inside the ear.

Hearing aid A small device worn behind or inside the ear that can make sound louder.

Induction loops A sound system in a building that sends signals to deaf people's hearing aids so they can hear announcements.

Lip-read To know what someone is saying by watching the shapes their lips make when they speak.

Microphone A small device that picks up sound.

Pitch The highness or lowness of a sound.

Profoundly deaf When someone is profoundly deaf, he or she hears very little.

Radio aid A device that can receive sounds spoken into a microphone and transmits them to a hearing aid.

Sign language To communicate by using hands in different positions to create letters and words.

Speech therapy Treatment that helps people learn to talk clearly.

Sign language interpreter Someone who explains to a hearing person what a deaf person is saying or the other way round.

Subtitles An information system that uses television to show words as well as pictures.

Textphone A special phone that allows people to communicate by typing in messages rather than speaking.

Videophones Telephone systems that use video as well as sound.

Further information

Learning Together by D. and J. Dowling (Dowling, 1990)
A finger spelling alphabet with signs for deaf and hearing children aged 2–7 years.

Think About Being Deaf by Maggie Woolley (Belitha, 1998)

When it's Hard to Hear by Judith Condon (Watts, 1998)
This book helps children think about what it means to be deaf, and how they would cope and communicate.

Look Hear (Lip Service, 1990).
A video introducing the basic skills of lip-reading.

BSL – A Guide for Beginners Book and Video Pack (BBC Books, 1988)
A useful visual resource for learning Stages 1 and 2 British Sign Language (BSL).

British Sign Language Works CD-ROM (Microbooks Ltd., 1997)
A multimedia guide to BSL.

You might like to look at these Internet sites:

• www.deafworldweb.org
This has a section called Deaf CyberKids with pen-pals, stories and information for deaf children.

• www.hipmag.org
An online magazine for deaf and hard-of-hearing kids and their friends with letters, news and stories.

The RNID library website is at:
www.ucl.ac.uk/UCL–Info/Divisions/Library/RNID

Index

Numbers in **bold** refer to pictures as well as text.